Seeing Beauty

Becoming Beautiful

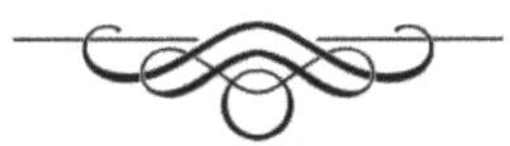

Indian Edition

Cover art by Nongkran Pornmingmas

For The Beautiful One
who makes us all beautiful.

Introduction

"We respond with joy to the call of beauty because in an instant it can awaken under the layers of the heart a forgotten brightness."
John O'Donohue

Our hearts long for a beautiful world.

Inside the soul there are memories of the beautiful world our hearts are longing for. Intuitively we know it is possible, which feeds our efforts to keep trying.

To create this beautiful world, we must develop a lens of beauty. The inner eye of the soul has the ability to perceive beauty between the bad news stories, sometimes hidden in private homes away **from** the public crises and breakdowns of our world.

This upheaval in our world has been created by human consciousness itself. We have forgotten to be conscious of our beautiful inner core. Now it is time to make this shift, to withdraw ourselves from the grossness of matter and look inside to our subtle natural self, the soul. This is the consciousness to awaken beauty in the world again.

As our eyes attune to beauty, we become the creators of a more beautiful world collectively. When the inner lens is attuned to beauty it activates the inner beauty of the soul.

In a world desperately in need of peace, some have questioned why, at this time, we have made beauty the focus of our attention.

Brahma Kumaris students worldwide are dedicated to creating a critical mass of consciousness, needed at this time to create a beautiful world. With guidance and power from the Divine Presence, we are gently and silently becoming more beautiful.

Golden Drops is a global initiative of the Brahma Kumaris contemplating the importance of our ability to see beauty in difficult times. The team who created it discovered that seeing beauty uplifts the human soul and improves the quality-of-life experience. We also noticed that seeing beauty acted as a bridge to noticing the beauty inside ourselves.

In this book, you will find a series of 31contemplations, reflective questions, meditations, and suggested experiences for you to contemplate the place of beauty in your life and awaken the beauty inside of you. There are QR codes visible for you to visit and experience the reflection point as a meditation commentary.

We begin with the Wisdom Behind Golden Drops as explained by several senior students of the Brahma Kumaris and a dear friend Deepak Chopra. QR codes are offered for you to listen to them speaking if you wish.

There are four parts, which flow into each other as a golden journey, with the aim to make a beautiful world manifest by you.

- **Seeing Beauty**
- **Touched by Beauty**
- **Inner Beauty**
- **Co-creating a Beautiful World**

Thank you for joining us on this 31-day journey which is actually the journey of a lifetime.

Thank you for adding more beauty to the world simply by contemplating beauty within yourself at this time.

"When we approach with reverence, great things decide to approach us. Our real life comes to the surface and its light awakens the concealed beauty in things. When we walk on the earth with reverence, beauty will decide to trust us. The rushed heart and arrogant mind lack the gentleness and patience to enter that embrace."

John O'Donohue, Beauty: The Invisible Embrace

Table of Contents

Golden Drops

Shining light on beauty
Consciously creating a beautiful world

The Wisdom Behind Golden Drops

Mohini Panjabi

Om Shanti

I am a peaceful soul.

The energy I create within myself fills my thoughts with power. Each thought then becomes a drop, a golden drop to create a beautiful world. We must first create this world within ourselves. Then every thought becomes a drop that contributes to a new creation. Through our thoughts, attitude and vision, we create a world of love, peace and harmony within ourselves. Then this world becomes visible outside.

Mohini Panjabi is the Additional Administrative Head of the Brahma Kumaris World Spiritual University

Jayanti Kirpalani

We invite you to share some thoughts, feelings, inspirations, ideas for a golden aged world, a world of truth, love, purity, and joy. There's a very special reason why we're inviting you to share a golden drop of beauty.

How do we make a beautiful world happen?

We have a very simple method. We know that if something is powerful enough in our thoughts, then it takes practical form in the world out there. And so, the invitation is to share many golden drops for a beautiful world.

The more we think, the more we speak, and the more we share these golden drops of beauty, we will actually make it happen. But of course, it's not just you alone. Share these ideas with your family, your friends and all those who might be interested in thinking about these things.

We had asked Dadi Gulzar, one of our most senior teachers, how long will it take to make a transition from the world as it is to the first moments of a new world. And her answer was "It will happen in a flash". This collective energy can bring things to a critical mass and a better world will come about in a flash.

Jayanti Kirpalani is the Additional Administrative Head of the Brahma Kumaris World Spiritual University

Deepak Chopra

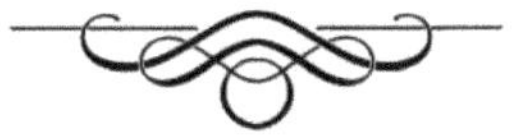

One of the best examples to understand collective transformation is the biological process called metamorphosis. This is when something like a caterpillar becomes a butterfly. The two are quite different, a caterpillar is like a worm, a butterfly is a very magical creature, with beautiful colours, that flies.

At a certain point in its development a caterpillar becomes very greedy. It starts to consume more than it needs and when its consumption exceeds its metabolic needs the caterpillar's body starts to die and liquify. But within the body of the caterpillar there are a few cells here and there that scientists refer to as the imaginal cells. Imaginal cells, because these imaginal cells are dreaming, a new reality, literally.

These imaginal cells vibrate in a different frequency of consciousness. And when the caterpillar's body recognizes these imaginal cells, it attacks them. The immune cells of the caterpillar attack the imaginal cells. But because the imaginal cells are vibrating at a different frequency, they remain immune to the onslaught.

Soon the immune cells give up and a critical threshold is reached. Then something magical happens. A gene, a genetic code that has been lying dormant in the body of the caterpillar, wakes up. And in that genetic code, is the information for wings.... is the information for a new heart ... the information for antennae, the information for legs... the information for a new metabolic rate because the metabolic rate of a flying creature has to be different from the metabolic rate of a worm.

All that is coded in the gene. And the gene which was sleeping wakes up because of the connectivity of the imaginal cells and as the rest of the body of the caterpillar starts to die, then the imaginal cells start to use the dying carcass of the caterpillar as their nutritive soup. Then a butterfly emerges with the flight to freedom.

You are the imaginal cells. So please, start to imagine the new reality….

Deepak Chopra

Charlie Hogg

We live in such an extraordinary world. Around 8 billion human beings. And some researchers tell us that each one of us emanates around 70,000 thought patterns in a waking day. It's almost like we're creating a collective thought soup.

When I tap into my true self, my original self, my spiritual essence, I begin to tap into the inner silence that is stored within me. This inner silence is a vibration, an energy, that heals, that nurtures, that restores and creates.

When my light of self awareness is switched on, I know who I am. Automatically, I start to radiate a different frequency. A frequency of silence and it is this vibration that starts to change the thought soup in the world. It starts to influence me. It begins to reach the material world and influence the material world. It reaches and influences our environment. It reaches and influences others.

So why not offer your golden drop? Just as our collective thoughts have created the atmosphere in the world now, our collective thoughts of this silence, this pure energy will begin to create a beautiful world.

Why not join us and add your drop of beauty to create the world we all have in our hearts?

Charlie Hogg

Neville Hodgkinson

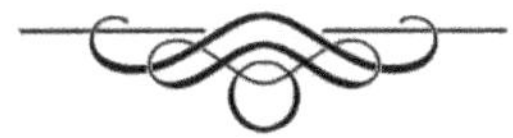

You may have noticed that when you walk through freshly fallen snow it makes it easier to pass that way again. The brain works in a very similar way. The energy of my every thought leaves an imprint within the brain.

When happy or sad feelings accompany the thought, those feelings also easily arise again, because brain cells that fire together, wire together. These mechanisms help me cope with the world in which I find myself.

What if I feel called to a more beautiful world?

Then, as much as I can, I must choose thoughts and feelings of beauty, of which scientists have found that the most powerful in rewiring the brain is love.

Neville Hodgkinson

Gopi Patel

What does it take to create real gold?

Amongst all the ornaments and jewelry that we see in today's world, there are grades of purity. The gold used to create the setting for an expensive jewel can be 16 karat gold or 14 karat gold. When gold has alloy mixed in it, its value decreases.

To transform gold into its purest state, it must be melted. Twenty-four karat gold is the purest and can be easily moulded into a new shape, creating something new.

We are living in a world filled with alloy. And, like gold, the only way to remove this is the melt it in the furnace of spiritual peace, power, and love.

In meditation, I allow the images, the noise, the thoughts of this old world to melt away and out of that furnace of deep peace and pure love I create a pure thought.

This is the golden drop needed for a new world.

Gopi Patel

BK Shivani

Golden drops … just the word itself creates a divine energy within.

But what are these golden drops? They are our every thought, our every feeling and intention, our vibration, which doesn't just remain here within, but radiates into the world and becomes a part of the collective consciousness of the planet.

It becomes a part of the global vibrational frequency, like a family of four in a house. What is the vibration, the energy of that home? It is the state of mind of those four minds in the house.

What is the vibration of the planet? It is the state of mind of all of us, the millions, and billions of us on this planet. It is the state of our minds, which creates the state of the world.

Today if anyone asked us, "What change do you want to see in the world?" We are very clear; we are waiting for a beautiful world. A world where there is harmony, unity, acceptance, compassion, unconditional love, peace, and happiness.

The spiritual equation reveals that our thoughts create our world, because thoughts don't remain inside, they vibrate, they radiate, and they become a part of the energy of the planet. Just like, my vibrations create the energy of my home.

So, the world that we want to see on the planet is what we need to create here within. Just take a pause and ask yourself, "To create that world, which everyone is waiting for, am I ready to create a little shift within?

People will not always be my way, situations will not always be my way, but my response, my thought, my vibration towards the situation, the person, towards the challenges and the crisis that's coming in my life, can my response be a response of calm, stability, forgiveness, letting go, kindness, compassion, or acceptance? And when I create that response, it's my golden drop.

This golden drop is not just going to make me feel very easy and comfortable within, it's not just going to give me a divine experience, but the golden drops of my vibrations, are going to radiate and raise the vibration of the planet and that will create the shift in the energy of the planet.

If the family of four are tense and disturbed, just one out of that four needs to shift by taking charge of their feelings to create feelings of stability, composure, peace, and the energy of the house will change. Just by one changing, because that one change will influence other minds and the vibration of the house will change.

So, a small percentage of the world population is needed, which is called the tipping point. This will influence the rest of the minds of the planet and will change the vibration of the world. So, are we ready to be a part of that tipping point which is needed to change the state of the world? Not just creating a better world but a beautiful, divine, golden world.

Let us begin. It's very simple. We've been waiting, wanting, hoping, wishing. Now its about creating just a shift within.

BK Shivani

PART I

Seeing Beauty

1

Beauty as Depth

Today is my first step into exploring my relationship with beauty. I consider the beauty that is deeper and more enduring than can be found in the superficial aesthetic or temporary style. True beauty lies deeper than the surface. It is an expression of the quality of the essence of a thing or person. This deeper beauty is not a tangible thing but is perceived by the inner eye. In a person, it reflects the personality and virtues inside. The inner eye is connected to universal truth and goodness and can discern the elevated things of life.

Reflective Question

How do you know the difference between superficial and deeper beauty?

Beauty as Depth

ACTIVITY

Choose something you can see from where you sit - an object, a picture or something in nature.

- Name one external aspect of the object that attracts you to the 'thing'. Name it.
- Now sit gazing at the 'thing' in a silent, meditative state and connect with the inner beauty of the 'thing' and see its essence. Name it.
- Reflect further on the difference between superficial and deep beauty.

Give thanks for the external beauty that draws your attention and for the internal essence that will stay with you.

My reflections for today:

Meditation

2

Permission to See Beauty

I give myself permission to see beauty because it increases my inner strength and joy in life. It is okay to see beauty even in a world where ugliness exists. My potential for creating something new begins with my ability to see beauty. I choose to open my inner door, to perceive the subtle beauty around me through what I see, hear, smell, taste or catch as a vibration. I simply allow myself to perceive it and experience it fully.

Reflective Question

What enables me to perceive beauty in the world around me?

Permission to See Beauty

ACTIVITY

Everyone gets a Beauty Detection Device (BDD) at birth.
Choose any moment today and consciously switch on your BDD.

- As you experience the moment, make note of the beauty only you can see with your BDD.
- What is the catalyst that turns on the switch for your personal BDD?

You carry your special, unique BDD with you always, use it as often as possible in a day.

My reflections for today:

Meditation

3

Life's Gifts of Beauty

Life wants to give me beauty. As human beings, we are embraced by Mother Nature and the elements. She offers air, water, food, and support for my living. When I look carefully, I can perceive the ways in which life is seeking to give me beauty. Then I can accept life's gifts.

Reflective Question

In what ways is life giving me the gift of beauty?

Life's Gifts of Beauty

ACTIVITY

Mother Nature gave you a gift of beauty today. How did you receive it?

- With your eyes? Or your ears? Or your sense of smell? Or your lungs? Or your stomach, your heart, your hands, or some of other part of your physical being?
- What was Mother Nature's gift to you today? Did you take in the beauty of that gift?

Take a moment now to give thanks for the beauty of the gift(s) you received.

My reflections for today:

Meditation

4

The Beauty of Connections

When I live in tune with life, patterns of beauty begin to emerge as moments of synchronicity. I catch these moments of unforeseen connections between people and events. Like an incognito tapestry, these moments create a subtle dance of beauty. When I become aware of these patterns, I stop and marvel with a sense of joy. Life has given me a special gift, letting me know that I am in tune with it. Noticing synchronicity is beautiful.

Reflective Question

What beauty do I see in the patterns and connections in my life?

The Beauty of Connections

ACTIVITY

You are connected.

- Take a moment to step outside the scene of your life and reflect on your recent experiences.
- Observe the pattern of energetic threads that connect the people, places, objects, utensils, animals, space in your life.
- Become aware of the fact that YOU are the connector between all the elements!

Thank each element of the scene for its beauty before you move back into the day.

Today as you go about your daily routine, take a moment to step outside the scene in your life and notice the threads of connections.

My reflections for today:

Meditation 

5

The Habit of Seeing Beauty

Seeing beauty becomes my natural, daily state of mind when I direct myself to consciously see it. By focusing my attention on beauty, I activate the discerning part of me. Then I develop the habit of seeing it. This shapes the lens of my awareness, so I begin to see more and more beauty. Then my mind is filled with this experience.

Reflective Question

How can I develop the habit of seeing more beauty?

The Habit of Seeing Beauty

ACTIVITY

You know what makes someone or something beautiful to you.

- Name at least three aspects that have been present for you in the past when you have discerned beauty.
- You have a habit of seeing beauty when these three elements are present.
- Today add 3 new elements of beauty and look for these new elements in addition to the original ones.

You are expanding your habit of seeing beauty.

My reflections for today:

Meditation

6

An Open Mind

In daily life, beauty is constantly crossing my path but sometimes I am not able to perceive it. When my mind is foggy it is like wearing unclean glasses, through which I cannot see clearly. Or having earplugs that block the sound of music, or a clothespin on my nose, so I miss the fragrance of flowers. When I am relaxed, my mind opens and suddenly I can experience the vibrant colors, textures and sounds of beauty around me.

Reflective Question

How do I keep my mind receptive to perceive beauty?

An Open Mind

ACTIVITY

Today is a good day to re-connect with one of your senses. Allow each sense to open your mind to beauty.
For this experiment, choose one from the following list:

- 3 spices from your spice cabinet (olfactory sense) or,
- 3 pieces of instrumental music (auditory sense) or,
- 3 vibrantly coloured flowers (visual sense).

Use the sense you have chosen to appreciate the finer qualities within the 3 specimens – How are they similar? Different? Compatible? Or better on their own?

Appreciate the wonder of this sense and how it allows your mind to be receptive to perceive beauty.

My reflections for today:

Meditation

7

Fresh Vision

When on holidays, away from daily life, I look at the world through new eyes. With a keen appreciation of detail, I perceive my surroundings as if for the first time and give myself a chance to experience their beauty. My ordinary, mundane vision suddenly becomes special. Sparkles of appreciation enter my mind. I realize that I am the one who chooses what to perceive and how.

Reflective Question

Where does beauty appear when I look at my world through fresh eyes?

Fresh Vision

ACTIVITY

Today put a picture from a past holiday or special scene in front of you (in your mind, or physically.)

- Notice the main subject(s) of the photo for just a second.
- Now shift your vision to the details that surround the main subject. Look in the corners and behind the main subject.
- Choose a new focus of beauty in the picture. Consider what it gives to the main subject (how it supports the main subject).

Let the beauty that surrounds the subject sparkle in your mind - creating a fresh vision.

My reflections for today:

Meditation

Seeing Beauty

You have begun your journey into beauty by recognizing its presence.

As you begin to tune the lens of your inner eye, something shifts inside, enabling you to create pleasing scenes on the screen of your mind.

When you choose to see beauty, you enter a new frequency. This helps the world to shift into newness.

What is your experience of these first 7 themes?

PART II

Touched by Beauty

8

Perceiving

I am the first to experience the benefit of beauty when I see it. Subtle feelings of beauty that sit quietly in the soul are awakened. My thoughts become more positive, my mood upgrades and my attention fills with appreciation. I begin to notice how beauty touches me.

Reflective Question

What happens inside of me when I see beauty?

Perceiving

ACTIVITY

This is an experiment we invite you carry out with one or two like-minded friends. Choose a moment when you are in conversation to take note of how you feel.

- Quietly name that feeling to yourself.
- Then let your friends know you are doing an experiment on beauty and ask everyone to take a minute, look around and note something of beauty in the world around you.
- Invite each one to share the 'thing of beauty' they perceived and let the conversation continue.
- For yourself, note your feeling after everyone has shared.

Receive the joy generated by the experience: more positive thoughts, better mood, appreciation of what was perceived (you may engage your friends in this part too!).

My reflections for today:

Meditation 

9

Lifted Above

It inspires me to reach higher than my ordinary existence. Going to the opera, the art gallery, while listening to music or walking in nature, I experience the gift of beauty. This lifts me above the mundane aspects of life as I connect with my pure inner core and feel lighter.

Reflective Question

How does beauty lift me above the ordinary?

Lifted Above

ACTIVITY

This week add an intentional moment of beauty to your daily routine, at least once a day. It may be:

- Viewing nature or art
- Listening to music or a friend's voice over the phone
- Savouring a favorite taste treat
- Sitting quietly in a room filled with your favorite scent

In these moments you are gifting yourself with beauty.
Enjoy the gift of a lift. And enjoy the lift of the gift of beauty!

My reflections for today:

Meditation

10

Feelings

I am touched by beauty. My mind is moved by the feelings created by beauty. Feelings are the deeper invisible currents that influence me. They fill my mind and carry me through life. I can use the experience of beauty to create positive waves in my mind. Then I am moved in positive directions.

Reflective Question

What feelings move me when I perceive beauty?

Feelings

ACTIVITY

Recall times in your life when you became aware of the beauty in you and around you.

- You are able to remember these times because beauty created feelings that filled you and moved you in a positive direction.
- You carry beauty in you.
- Today appreciate the waves of beauty that you have captured in your mind.

They are yours and no one can take them away from you.

My reflections for today:

Meditation 

11

A Well Mind

Seeing beauty awakens a sense of awe and wonder in me. Even for a moment, this experience gives a boost to my mental health. I begin to appreciate, admire, wonder, and give value to things around me. Just being in this state of mind, increases my strength, hope, and resilience.

Reflective Question

How does beauty affect my mental state?

A Well Mind

ACTIVITY

Try this experiment to test how your mental state can affect your physical state.
Ask a friend to help with the test as described here.

- Stand comfortably and raise your left arm out to shoulder level parallel to the floor.
- Think about something that you are confused or nervous about. In this state of thought ask your friend to apply pressure to push your arm down at the forearm, while at the same time you should attempt to keep your arm extended in the same position. Notice what happens.
- Now take a deep breath and think about a beautiful, treasured memory you hold in your heart. Extend your arm again in this state of thought and ask your friend to repeat the pressure test.

Note the level of strength in the two experiments and appreciate every positive thought created by your well mind is supporting your physical health.

My reflections for today:

Meditation

12

Beyond Trauma

Beauty touches the wholeness inside of me. Even if I am living with the experience of wounds or trauma, beauty connects me to a place of health inside. I identify with this intact core of wholeness.

Reflective Question

What is the experience of wholeness?

Beyond Trauma

ACTIVITY

Today imagine your life as a beautiful picture, capturing a momentary scene that makes your life beautiful.

- Now in your mind transform the beautiful scene into a puzzle of many pieces.
- There is one empty spot in the puzzle and a small puzzle piece lying outside the beautiful picture. Notice the place inside the puzzle where this piece fits.
- Consider this small puzzle piece to be a wounded part of yourself.
- Consider the empty spot in the puzzle to be the safe place for this wounded part of you to sit.
- Place the wounded piece safely inside the larger picture of your life.

Placing the piece in this spot feels right and allows you to feel whole inside … so there is no longer a feeling of emptiness, pain, or regret. Where the edges meet, imagine sealing them with gold filling, creating an even more beautiful picture. This repairs you internally and you breath wholeness and health into your being. You are whole.

My reflections for today:

Meditation 

13

Immune Boost

My body responds to beauty. The intricate series of interconnections that make up my immune system are nourished by the positive state of mind created when I see beauty. This higher vibration supports physical health.

Reflective Question

How does my body respond when I see beauty?

Immune Boost

ACTIVITY

Stand, wherever you are right now.

- Take a deep breath and look down around your feet, see the beauty hidden there.
- Now bring your head up, chin parallel to the floor, take another deep breath and look straight ahead. Find beauty hidden in front of you.
- Take a deep breath and make a quarter turn to your right. See the new scene in front of you – locate something of beauty hidden there.
- Take another deep breath and continue with another quarter turn to the right. Appreciate beauty that you catch a glimpse of here.
- Take another deep breath and turn once more a quarter turn to the right and close your eyes, feel something of beauty inside you.
- Take one more deep breath to complete your turn, then tilt your head back and look up. Connect with the Divine.

As you sit down again, know that every cell and connection in your immune system is nourished by the beauty you see around you, returning you to good health.

My reflections for today:

Meditation

14

Harmonious Composition

When I perceive harmony, it affects me. Beauty is experienced when separate elements combine in harmonious composition. A combination of form, colour, sight, sound, taste, and touch resonate within me as beauty.

Reflective Question

How does the experience of harmony affect me?

Harmonious Composition

ACTIVITY

Today you are invited to experiment by creating or remember having created a harmonious composition - perhaps a veggie tray, a meal, a craft project, a new outfit!
If you are in creation mode, choose a variety of different aspects for the composition; if you are remembering a recent creation reflect on the different aspects that you combined – could be:

- Colours
- Forms
- Tastes
- Sounds
- Textures

We create beauty when all these differences unite in pleasing harmony. Share your composition or the memory of it, with a friend and describe how this harmonious composition affects you through your senses – vision, taste, sound, and so on. Have fun!

My reflections for today:

Meditation

Touched by Beauty

You have silently witnessed the awakening of your natural wholeness. By focusing on beauty, you have begun to see how true healing is not far away ~ for yourself and so for the world.

Describe your experience of this theme and what you have discovered about your natural wholeness.

What beauty touched you that made this healing happen?

PART III

Inner Beauty

15

Discover Me

In the core of my inner being, lies the natural beauty of my essence. Sometimes it feels hidden, but it is always there. My essence is naturally shaped from the qualities, the virtues and the special energy that is me. I take time to discover me. I sit with myself and become more aware of the beauty within me.

Reflective Question

What is the natural beauty of my essence?

Discover Me

ACTIVITY

Today take 5 minutes to explore the essence that has shaped you. Sit and study your hands. Like fingerprints, your hands are uniquely yours and what you do with your hands is unique to your personality and story. You might think of activities done with your hands such as making bread, or writing, or creating anything. It often feels like there is something inside you that wants to come out, to be expressed through your hands into the world, to give the best of you to the world, to make it a better place. It is very valuable to start experiencing this as you move your hands.

- Identify one quality that lies deep within you, that moves your hands (to do what they do).
- Identify the intention behind what your hands do.
- Identify the special energy that radiates from your hands that is uniquely yours.

Thank both hands with a namaste or prayer gesture that touches your forehead, your lips, and your heart.

My reflections for today:

Meditation

16

Untouched Me

In the awareness of my inner world, I experience the purest part of myself. This part of me has never been touched by the outside world. It is sacred and eternal. Even when I am not aware of it, this quiet innocent part of me gives rise to beauty. I am touched by the beauty in me.

Reflective Question

How does my own beauty touch me?

Untouched Me

ACTIVITY

Take time to recognize the sacred, eternal innocent part of you that gives rise to your beauty.

- Sit quietly with a piece of paper and pencil in front of you. Write 5-6 roles you play in life on this paper.
- Now turn the paper over and draw a big heart on this side of the paper.
- Thinking about the roles on the back side of the paper, identify 1-2 gifts (inner qualities, special powers – like your superpower) that lie deep in your heart that allow you to play each role.
- Fold the paper in half like a book so the heart is hidden inside.
- Holding the folded 'paper heart' in front of your physical heart, now open the folded paper to reveal your heart to the world outside. Then close it.
- Repeat this slowly 3 times.
- Observe how the core of you is protected and safe, ready to be opened when, and as you wish.

When you have completed your 'heart of gifts', make a plan to visit one of your gifts each day and give thanks to this deep core of you that allows you to play your part, and that only you can visit.

My reflections for today:

Meditation

17
Attuning

My inner beauty can be hidden from me. Sometimes others see my beauty more than I do. When my relationship with myself is loving, I begin to see the beauty inside of me. Then it becomes more visible to others. Seeing my own beauty attunes me to the inner beauty in others. Beauty awakens beauty.

Reflective Question

How does my beauty attune to the beauty in others?

Attuning

ACTIVITY

Today imagine you are driving on a 2-way highway, with cars going past you from the other direction. You have your headlights on, so others can see you.

- For every car you meet, you recognize a 'quality' of their 'headlights', as virtues shining brightly or dimmed.
- Think of these virtues as characteristics of the people driving toward you today.
- Name the qualities/virtues you see in them.

Next, recognize that they see that same light (virtue) shining in you.
Today imagine 'turning' on your lights (virtues, qualities) that will encourage others to turn on theirs.

My reflections for today:

Meditation

18

Virtue Palette

My attitude and vision are an expression of my personality. The colour code of my inner beauty is a palette of virtues that are expressed through my eyes, in my behavior, and in my words. Each expression is an act of instantaneous art, so unique for each person, so unique for me.

Reflective Question

What palette of virtues am I expressing in my life?

Virtue Palette

ACTIVITY

This week colour your world with virtues – personal qualities of the soul. Look around your world from where you are sitting right now. Notice the colours in your environment, including your clothing. Each time you see a colour, check the list below for its virtue expression.

- Dark Blue for BLISS
- Medium Blue for WISDOM/TRUTH
- Light Blue for PEACE
- Green for LOVE
- Orange for PURITY
- Yellow for HAPPINESS
- Red for POWER

Notice which colours resonated with you the most. Claim that virtue or quality as the signature 'colour' of your personality.

My reflections for today:

Meditation

19

Back to Self

What I find beautiful brings me back to my own qualities. I am attracted to certain images, styles, designs, home furnishings, art, and music. I find these things attractive because their qualities resonate with something inside of me. It awakens something in me. A special part of me opens up ~ my own beauty.

Reflective Question

What beauty surrounds me in this moment and how is it a reflection of my inner beauty?

Back to Self

ACTIVITY

Today you are invited to sit for 10-15 minutes in one of your favorite spots. (If you can't physically be there, recreate it in your mind or sit with a picture).

- Study the details of the 'spot' – the shapes, colours, designs, contrasts, complementariness, repeating pattens, and so on. Check what you notice about the features of this 'spot'.
- Identify at least five elements you find attractive in the spot.
- Consider the qualities that are expressed by the elements you have chosen.

These qualities are also in you.
Give thanks to the beauty outside that attracts you to your favorite spot. It reflects your inner beauty.

My reflections for today:

Meditation

20

Beholder's Eye

I am one who can behold beauty. I am one who can recognize beauty. In this way, beauty needs me. It needs my inner eye. I am one of the beholders, whose eyes can treasure, appreciate, and admire every single drop of beauty. From the seat of my inner beauty, I perceive the beauty that exists around me.

Reflective Question

What is the power of one who beholds beauty?

Beholder's Eye

ACTIVITY

Imagine your least favorite season of the year.

- Identify at least one aspect of that season that does not appeal to you.
- Now behold that season and this aspect with the eye of the beholder of beauty – with this eye everything you see holds beauty!
- Refresh your attitude toward this season by treasuring, appreciating and admiring this special aspect of beauty that only your new eyes are attuned to see.

Give thanks.

My reflections for today:

Meditation

21

Act of Gratitude

Beauty has always been part of my life. My life is an expression of the beauty in me. Naturally I bring my virtues and qualities into the practical creation of everything in my life; cooking, building, moving, gardening, etc. To create is to bring the best of my inner self into a unique form, as a pure gift to the world. This is an act of gratitude to life itself.

Reflective Question

Today what is my act of gratitude to life?

Act of Gratitude

ACTIVITY

Today you are invited to create an imaginary bouquet of your 'inner flowers' i.e. your virtues.

- In your mind, choose flowers of different heights to represent your virtues - one to stand tall (a thriller – its beauty thrills you every time it is revealed), one to spill over the sides (a spiller – the beauty of this virtue is that it is always there for you, spilling out of you naturally), and one to fill in between (a filler – the beauty of this virtue always fills you with joy)!
- Feel the beauty as you "choose" the flowers that represent the beauty of the virtues in you.
- Touch the beauty in you as you present this bouquet to the Divine, to yourself, or to a friend.

Be grateful to life for giving you the experience of beauty in this beautiful bouquet of virtues.

My reflections for today:

Meditation

Inner Beauty

You have embraced beauty in your pure core. You are willing to dive deeper and deeper within. By seeing, hearing and feeling it, you give life to beauty. Thus, beauty outside needs you to so it can exist. Life has invited you to offer your inner beauty to it.

What have you discovered about your inner beauty that you can offer with love to increase beauty in the world?

PART IV

Co-Creating a Beautiful World

22

Attitude of Co-Creation

Dear friend, are you aware that you are constantly in a process of co-creation? Every thought, word and action adds to life's creation. By being attuned to everything and everyone as a companion, you live with an attitude of co-creating a beautiful world. Attentive to every moment, every encounter, every situation as an opportunity to add beauty to our world, you invite life to create this with you. By offering your inner richness, you invite life to co-create with you.

Reflective Question

Am I aware of my role as a co-creator of the world?

Attitude of Co-Creation

ACTIVITY

Today you are invited to consciously step into your role as a co-creator of the world.
It may be a moment when you:

- Think a beautiful thought and send that thought out to the world, or
- Offer a word to a friend that describes the beauty they bring into the world, or
- Act in a way that adds a moment of comfort to the lives of the souls around you.

Review your role as a co-creator at the end of the day and give thanks.
Repeat with a new contribution each day.

My reflections for today:

Meditation

23

A New Consciousness

Dear friend, are you aware that the cracks we see in the world around us are evidence of something new breaking open? Can you feel that a new consciousness is emerging from the old? It is a spiritual awakening, a collective shift of consciousness, coming from the human spirit and the energy of virtues and values. This newly emerging consciousness holds the promise of a beautiful world.

Reflective Question

How does a new consciousness, based on virtues and values, co-create a beautiful world?

A New Consciousness

ACTIVITY

Today sit with an image of the world in your mind.

- Imagine the very best of humanity's virtues and values being showered on all living beings on the earth.
- Imagine those same virtues and values rising like steam from the inner core of the earth.
- See all earthly beings absorbing these beautiful virtues and awakening to a new reality on the earth.
- As you continue to move through your day, continue to let these images shape how you see everyone and everything around you.

You are co-creating a new consciousness for a new reality and a new world.

My reflections for today:

Meditation

24

Today I Imagine...

Dear friend, did you know that the mind follows a picture? First, a picture must come alive in your mind before it can become a reality in the outer world. Your contribution to co-create a beautiful world begins with vivid pictures in your mind. Can you see the picture of the beautiful world your heart is longing for? What wholeness do you want for our world? As you begin to imagine a beautiful world, you become a partner in the design of such a world. And the interesting thing is ~ by imagining it, your companions in co-creation begin to awaken, they become ready to make it manifest with you.

Reflective Question

What pictures can I create of a beautiful world?

Today I Imagine...

ACTIVITY

Today you are invited to look at the following scenes and ask your heart, *"what would this same space look like if it was soaked in thoughts of beauty?"* With your mind, add a touch of beauty to each of the following scenes. Check:

- The indoor space surrounding where you are sitting right now
- An external/ outdoor space that can be observed from where you are, perhaps through a window or doorway
- The inner space that is you, an eternal soul
- The space between who you really are and your expression in the external world

Click a picture of these 'touched up' spaces – filled with the beauty of love from your heart. Carry these spaces of 'touched up' beauty with you today and make them real!

My reflections for today:

Meditation

25

Collective Consciousness

Dear friend, are you ready to create what you are longing for? We are longing to create a beautiful world, together. Today the world has many intelligent people with many brilliant ideas to improve our world. What the world needs now is the collective energy of unity, cooperation, and commitment to carry these inspirations into fruition. As the collective consciousness shifts in the direction of what we want to create, suddenly the collective power tips the world to a new expression. So let us tune into the collective consciousness by opening our hearts and minds.

Reflective Question

Where can I tune into the collective consciousness and our shared desire for a beautiful world?

Collective Consciousness

ACTIVITY

Today invite a like-minded friend or family member to go for a walk with you or to visit for a cup of tea/coffee. During your time together, open your heart and mind, and sprinkle your conversation with some of the following themes:

- Unity you've seen in the world – collective activities that brought beauty into the world.
- Cooperation you've experienced with others this week.
- Commitment of souls to be their best and how they expressed themselves in the world.

Give thanks for this conversation and know it has shifted your consciousness and that of the soul you were in conversation with.

My reflections for today:

Meditation

26

Co-Create with Other People

Today I welcome other people as my companions in co-creating a beautiful world. I offer my inner richness in the form of virtues and values and observe what happens when I listen, work, and meet other people. What is the energy between us, what opens in me and the other? What beauty do we co-create and how does it add to the world? My interactions with other people contribute to the beautiful world my heart is longing for. Today let me be consciously aware of co-creating beauty with the people in my life.

Reflective Question

How can I co-create a beautiful world with the people I meet today?

Co-Create with Other People

ACTIVITY

Today plan to spend time with someone to create something beautiful together for others. It might be:

- Painting hearts on rocks to leave along a walkway or entrance to a hospital.
- Taking a garbage bag and cleaning up along the street or roadway where you live
- Creating a visual message that makes you smile and placing it outside where you live, to bring a smile to others
- Join a world meditation hour this Sunday

Share the beauty of the values and virtues in your heart in these interactions with your friend.

My reflections for today:

Meditation

27

Co-Create with Animals

Today I welcome animals as my companions in co-creating a beautiful world. Animals are present in our daily lives. There are birds, dogs, ducks, cats, deer, and other animals where I live. I notice them and allow them to entertain me through their eyes, their movements, and their sounds. I notice the feelings inside of me when I am with animals. I notice what feelings exist between us ~ of appreciation, friendship, companionship. I am aware of my relationship with animals and how it contributes to a beautiful world.

Reflective Question

What feelings do I have in relation to animals?

Co-Create with Animals

ACTIVITY

Take 10 minutes today to explore your relationship with animals.

- Imagine your 'favorite' animal sitting beside you right now – wild, tame, winged, finned – this animal is offering its cooperation by sharing a comfortable space with you – they know they are safe with you, no matter how strange the environment!
- As you imagine this animal with you, attune your movement to its movement – resting, looking ahead, eyes closing, a yawn escaping, stretching, and so on.
- You are in sync with your animal friend, and it feels beautiful.
- Recognize the special nature of this companionship.

Give thanks for the ability to co-create a beautiful moment in the world together. Bid your animal friend good-bye, 'til next time!

My reflections for today:

Meditation

28

Co-Create with Nature

Today I welcome nature as my companion in co-creating a beautiful world. Nature is a fascinating expression of the five elements: earth, water, fire, air and ether. Nature is full of variety. Every blade of grass, every branch, every stone, every dew drop, every volcano, all are an expression of nature. Nature invites me to relate to it, interact with it, and to co-create with it.

Reflective Question

How do I interact with nature to co-create a beautiful world?

Co-Create with Nature

ACTIVITY

It's a beautiful day. You take yourself outside to experience the five elements of nature. As you walk, look around you.

- Let your gaze fall on all that is natural, not human-made.
- Look, listen and feel its expressions.
- Feel the rain falling on you. (water)
- Notice the space between the raindrops. (ether)
- Feel the earth firmly beneath you. (earth)
- See the steam radiating off the warm earth, feel the heat of it. (fire)
- Smell the natural fragrances in the air. (air)

All of nature is co-creating feelings of beauty with you to share with your companions in the human and natural world.

My reflections for today:

Meditation 

29

Co-Create with Time

Today I welcome time as my companion in co-creating a beautiful world. Time is a treasure, an invisible gift of life. When I am aware of this, I can use time in such a way that it benefits the whole world. I just have to be attuned to the gift of every moment, while being present. I help myself to create golden moments of silence and withdraw myself for a while. I feel how my dear partner time wants me to create with it, so the outcome is good and beautiful for the whole.

Reflective Question

How can I play with time as my partner to co-create beauty in my life?

Co-Create with Time

ACTIVITY

Time has come to you wrapped as a beautiful gift of companionship. Take a few moments today to experience yourself sitting together silently with time, as friends. Allow yourself and time to be in sync:

- when you stop, time stops;
- when you move, time moves;
- when you create, time creates with you.

Smile at time and feel the warmth of your relationship with time, and together your vibrations soothe the world around you – co-creating a beautiful world.

My reflections for today:

Meditation 

30

Co-Create with Situations

Today I welcome all situations as my companions in co-creating a beautiful world. Challenges are constantly in front of me. There is no escape, only opportunities to make the best of every situation. With an attitude of co-creation, I am present in each moment to consciously listen to the hidden invitation, even within challenging situations. Life whispers to me, inviting me to co-create beauty, especially in situations that are not beautiful at all. With silence and a loving intention, I perceive the potential for beauty in every situation. In this way, I join life to co-create a beautiful world.

Reflective Question

How can I co-create beauty in my present life situations?

Co-Create with Situations

ACTIVITY

Imagine you are inside a situation that has caused you discomfort in the past. Imagine that this situation has come to honour something in you. Decide today to open your heart and mind to explore what this is.

- Knowing what the challenge looks like and feels like – comfort yourself with a moment of silence.
- Follow this with a loving intention to accept the gift of beauty this situation is offering you.
- Look deep, look hard, look lovingly at the situation.
- Find its hidden beauty.

Thank yourself for staying present and promise to exercise the same commitment to finding beauty in every situation, loving the beauty you co-create.

My reflections for today:

Meditation

31

The Impossible is Possible

Dear friend, thank you for being part of this Golden Drops initiative to shine light on beauty. Have you been able to appreciate the beauty within this initiative? Have you been able to bring closer the beautiful world your heart is longing for? It is on the threshold. Can you feel it? It is awakened by all of us as partners in co-creation. By paying attention to beauty, you have added positive energy to the mental health in the world. In this way, you are making the impossible possible by consciously creating a beautiful world. Life itself is deeply grateful to you. So farewell and receive greetings of peace and beauty from the heart of every living creature on earth. Together we are creating a new consciousness.

Reflective Question

What precious gift has Golden Drops brought to you? How can you share it with others?

The Impossible is Possible

ACTIVITY

After many days of bringing beauty into your life, you decide today to write a thank-you note to life itself.

- Find a beautiful spot to sit.
- Find a beautiful pen.
- Find beautiful paper.

Allow your gratitude to flow out of your heart, through your arm and hand, through the pen and onto the paper.

- Give thanks to this Golden Drops Initiative, to the beautiful world your heart is longing for.
- To all the partners in your co-creations of beauty.
- To all the positive energy you have co-created and received.
- To all the loving creatures on the earth who have helped co-create beauty.

Know that you are of a different consciousness now than you were a month ago. Know that you are ready to see and co-create beauty anywhere, anytime. It is all possible.

Close off your thank-you note with a heart, a smiley face and happily return to your beautiful world!

My reflections for today:

Meditation

Co-Creating a Beautiful World

Hopefully you have learned about yourself and discovered new corners of beauty inside of you. You are one of the creators of a wonderful new world.

What clear vision are you beginning to see for a beautiful world and how can you contribute to bring it into existence?

Thank you for joining us on this journey into beauty.
We hope you have enjoyed your time spent exploring beauty.

We welcome your comments to:
goldendrops@au.brahmakumaris.org

If you wish to pursue the journey of inner beauty even further, please check out a Brahma Kumaris meditation centre near you.

Golden Drops Playlist

The Lighthouse
Powered by the Brahma Kumaris

Brahma Kumaris Centre near you

About the Brahma Kumaris

- The Brahma Kumaris are a spiritual movement that originated in Hyderabad, Sindh, during the 1930s. The movement has distinguished itself from its Hindu roots and sees itself as a vehicle for spiritual teaching rather than as a religion.
- Over 8000 Meditation Centres in 125 countries- organization run by donation only.
- It is the largest spiritual movement led by women.
- An NGO with General Consultative Status with the United Nations Economic and Social Council.
- Purpose of the movement: to create a more peaceful world, one person at a time. The slogan is: *as I change, the world changes.*
- BK teaches a form of meditation called Raja Yoga that focuses on soul consciousness or the construct that our primary identity is that we're souls who live in bodies. In meditation we aim to connect to our inherent soul qualities: bliss, love, peace, power, purity.
- The Brahma Kumaris is oriented to service work worldwide in many forms: featuring many online and in person courses, retreats, etc. all free of charge.
- Philosophies for living are grounded in a sustainable approach to the environment and human relationships over the long term for the planet. Living lightly on the planet and the idea that when we feel fulfilled, people will naturally be inclined "take-less" materially, from the environment and from one another.
- The main Spiritual University Campus in India has capacity for 25,000 students which can all be fed 3 meals a day powered solely by solar generation.
- There is IQ, EQ, and SQ (spiritual intelligence) ~ SQ is what the BKs are about: teaching people how to become masters of their state of mind and how one can sustain their inherently enthusiastic, loving human spirit.

www.ingramcontent.com/pod-product-compliance
Lightning Source LLC
LaVergne TN
LVHW021158160826
845679LV00024B/2157

* 9 7 9 8 8 9 6 3 2 8 5 6 8 *